Book of Sparks

Psalms for a New World

Other Titles by Efrayim Levenson:

For My Relations
(Buffalo, NY: Poetrymanz, 2000)

Titles Found on Amazon:
Dances With Tears
(Hoboken, NJ: Poets Wear Prada, 2007)
Second Edition, 2009; Third Edition, 2013

Funhouse
(Hoboken, NJ: Poets Wear Prada, 2013)

Book of Sparks
Psalms for a New World

Efrayim Levenson

Waterloo Cottage Press · Far Rockaway, New York

Book of Sparks: Psalms for a New World
Copyright ©2014 Efrayim Levenson

Waterloo Cottage Press®
1415A Waterloo Place
Far Rockaway, New York 11691

First North American Publication 2014
First Mass Market Paperback Edition 2014

This book is typeset in Adobe® Frutiger Medium Condensed and Coniglio Type® Market Ltd / Trailer Park Numerals

Spark 2, 3, 4, 5, 9, 11, 12, 15, 18, and 19 appeared originally in Chabad of Rego Park's Poetry Corner

Spark 3, 5, 7, 9, 10, and 19 appeared previously in Dances With Tears (Hoboken, NJ: Poets Wear Prada, 2007 and 2013)

Spark 6 appeared originally in Respuestas:
The Neruda Project
http://nerudaproject.wordpress.com/2010/08/27/563/

Spark 16 appeared originally in What Happens Next? #34
(New York, NY: Eve Packer, 2011)

Spark 17 appeared originally in Poetica Magazine:
Reflections of Jewish Thought
(Norfolk, VA: Poetica Publishing Company, 2009)

ISBN-10: 0615969771
ISBN-13: 978-0615969770

Join us on Facebook at Efrayim Levenson. https://www.facebook.com/efrayim.levenson
Written correspondence regarding this title may be sent to efrayimlevenson@gmail.com

PUBLISHED BY WATERLOO COTTAGE PRESS®
PRINTED IN THE USA BY CREATESPACE, AN AMAZON COMPANY
For Orders by U.S. trade bookstores and wholesalers, please visit www.amazon.com

Dedicated to
the Blessed Memory of

Annette Marcia Levenson
(Chana bas Avraham)

Irwin Leon Levenson
(Yitzchak Leib ben Hershel HaLevi)

A special Thank You goes out to the following for their support in making this offering possible: Rabbi Eli Blokh, Rabbi Yossi Halberstam, Rabbi Yossi Mendelson, Shawn Martin and Joseph V. Coniglio.

1

Wake up! The day march is on! It's Redemption Day! We're free, redeemed of our slavery to our restrictions. It's Redemption Day! Pack your belongings. Pack their gifts. There's a perilous road home just outside these gates. Don't be afraid. G-d's Will and wisdom is your guiding hand. The terrain is rough, filled with pits, Amalekis and broken glass. We will make it together, together with Him. It's Redemption Day! Our freedom to perform commandments is our freedom from the ties that bind. Hurry! Hurry, before the soul of the animal within has time to protest. Now is the time to free us of the leaven that inflates the everyday. We need to be flat, nullified, and moldable for the love of G-d to enter us like our only breath. It's Redemption Day! The taste doesn't need to be bitter anymore. Tonight our tears can be as sweet as the Four Cups of joy we drink. It's Redemption Day!

2

My thanks for a new day rises with the sun. I offer thanks to G-d. Our way is lit by the promise of the living and eternal King. Happy mornings in prayer are beauty reborn with He who has provided me with my every need. My head and arm are wrapped in bands of leather meditation. I take upon myself to Hear, O Israel. Now I'm prepared to face the dance of the world, head above heart in joyful calmness. Will you come with me? You need only say "yes" and G-d will lead your way to leave the shackles of constriction behind, one day at a time.

3

As the sun rises over the tree line children of G-d are thankful for another chance to breathe the wealth of His Kindness, till the field of His Righteousness, sow the produce of His Truth. May I have this dance? The music of our lives is the rhythm of our souls, the best we can hope for on short notice. Love is the blood that courses through our veins of faith, the song that soothes nightmares. Dance with me. It's my last chance to show what 2 right feet can do. How do you love so much the incessant dichotomy that shares your bed? How hard must worlds collide before the chaff falls away? How soft must kisses be before they pierce stone? May I have this hoedown dance? Maybe the band will play a swinging shuffle next. Just don't bop your head off before you lay it down to rest, to pray, to dream of a peaceful home, a hideaway from the frenzy. The dance steps are lighter, more agile and free on the mountain where silence breathes a smile. Come dance on the mountaintop with me.

4

Swing your Image of G-d down to the comfy chairs to hear this boogie that shuffles off to I forget where. No illusions there, no visions either. I remember how your life of age-lessness committed the crime of perpetual youth, happy with your sadness. Waltz on over to clean breathing in clear thought and listen to His Presence proclaim "I am here!" to tango with you through the thickness of the night, the thin-ness of the morning light.

5

I rise above the smoke and ash in the easy rhythm of your love's embrace. The stars' twinkle in your eyes releases me from the noise in the void. Lie with me on the forest's floor. We'll sing psalms to Heaven, melodies to the Light of Infinite Oneness, and laugh with the birds' replies. The sun in our hearts shines through the heavy threat of snow white clouds. You touch me in the air we breathe. I hear your soul call from miles away. Come home to me. Come home.

6

I give thanks for each morning's new fire in a shower of abundance. The thundercloud cries as it asks the parched earth for forgiveness for being away so long.

7

I will dance under a rain-filled sky and dream of sun-soaked sand that buries my footprints as I walk home to peace in a quiet heart that sings of everything 6 strings can give to a life in need of the nurture of a pipe enemies can smoke as friends on a free bridge to the depths of joy where we swim together in love with the music of a perfect day.

8

Hope is the shadow that guides our way through the ceaseless rain on a whim of flight to a House of Pure Rhythm in the rising light. The crow calls from sunburst waves, outside this air-conditioned cave, to wake us for prayer this morning, louder than sweet nothings whispered in the left ears of our snoring. The week winds down, falls into His arms, to rest once again in the caress of Songs of Thanks for miracles hidden, blessings revealed, in progress reflected, as we seek three: G-d, you, and me.

9

Tomorrow will sparkle in preparation for Shabbat, a prelude to harmony, a song at the edge of bliss. Here comes the Queen, her crown of radiance protected by a snood.

10

The world is in here, G-d out there. One and the same are miles apart. Changes don't reconcile every day. I am alone with you, alone, the space between togetherness. And yet I try to live without a cloud encompassing. If only this window faced the black west, sometimes blue. If I cried my tears would sound like yours. A guitar with no strings remembers how to sing. Love endures a mouth faster than eyes, a mind quicker than pen, a smiling portrait of decay. Incomplete Prosperity is my name in rare places. I am a shell that shines, brighter than wickedness, much less than intermediacy. If we wash our hands and breathe our psalm our love becomes answered prayer. If we don't we give birth to an empty, questioned soul.

11

Take this man and turn him into songs that dance for You to the music You put in his heart. He wants to hear the words You write there. Will his eyes know what to listen to first? He wants to hitch a ride on Your chariot to Heaven before it's too late. Please take him with You to Redemption. Exile's sinister smile lurks around every corner. Peace in his heart comes in such small pieces. Only You, G-d, can provide the glue to make him whole.

12

Mary ate some shredded lamb. Was there approval? No. And everywhere that Mary went her transgression was sure to go. Her grandmother waited 6 hours between the kid and its mother's feta. But that's so "old school" in these days of fast-food souvlaki, where our communities change rabbis like underpants and applaud giving Holy Land to our enemies. And everywhere that Harry went the law was sure to blow. The master of return's path is a winding maze toward the reward of contracted light. Won't you follow him through the trials of fire and water to the perfection of commandments and love of Israel? G-d is awaiting your arrival.

13

Behind eyes heavy with sleep there is a dream of undecipherable ceremonies and hidden miniature libraries. Don't forget to wake me for dinner. Your kosher delicacies are a symphony for my taste buds. My tongue waltzes with my teeth for your sustenance, fruits of the ground, and everything that was created through His words. Yum! Is it time for blessings already? And tomorrow? Tomorrow I will thrive on food my soul can wear, an edible garment for my thought, speech and action. It attaches me to G-d's Will and wisdom, one call up, one teaching, one psalm at a time. It gives me the strength, the shield and the armor to perform His commandments, to help prepare the world for the Messiah's arrival.

14

Walk off cliff to climb the mountain. G-d is the walk. G-d is the cliff. G-d is the fall. G-d is the fear. G-d is the bottom. G-d is the shoes. G-d is the climb. G-d is the cliff. G-d is the walk.

15

We afflict ourselves today and remember thousands of years of fallen brothers and sisters and hold our breath in anticipation of another decimation to our nation. Our physical connection to G-d's Presence has been destroyed in the squandering of our Exodus, the rubble of our Temples, our evictions from Spain, Britain, and the first trainload to Auschwitz. We pray for redemption today, ours but not the L-rd's. We will continue to win a losing battle until we ask in the right way. Then we will be given the return of His Presence in the hands and heart of the Messiah, to be placed on G-d's Holy Altar.

16

The head of foxes is a tail when lions come to feed on all that isn't known of truth. He hides in the thicket of those who are less, chest swelled, a soldier at attention. His humility is dressed in a many-colored coat of pride, and dares to believe his praised righteousness for so much incomplete service. Inside will never equal outside in a vacuum devoid of refinement.

17

Is your need to kill me for the love of G-d greater than my willingness to die for Him? Today is a better day to live but I am not afraid to be your enemy, for the love of G-d is my shield and armor. Through His eyes I see peace on the horizon, at the foot of the lowest mountain. 613 steps to the top I climb for the love of G-d, to put Him into His Dwelling. The fight of my life on this path to the Garden begins with surrender to His Will. For the love of G-d, today is a good day to die in battle with His enemy. Tomorrow the Messiah, the Savior, the King comes to bring lasting peace to our children, His children, for the love of G-d.

18

If one 45-year-old child voiced a prayer, and was joined by 4 more, it would be loud. If 16 more children spoke to G-d, and 64 more came along, it would be louder. If 144 adults listened to the chant, and sang along with 576 grandmothers and grandfathers, it would be deafening. If the child's prayer reached thousands, and millions raised their voices to the sky, it would be awakening. If the whole world shouted to Heaven, in just one voice, the child's prayer would be answered, and the Messiah would come.

19

The brightness of Your surf sings in that place in my soul where the past rides the wave of the future. Automatic men in my memory smile at the beauty of this hidden beach of stone. It's been a long time since I've been home among the noisemakers, drowning out the name of our malicious enemy of long ago. I can feel the first melody of my rebirth welling up in my chest, closed eyes rocking around the gathering table. Wine and stronger push us to our dancing feet and swinging arms, to enlighten our celebration of knowing no difference between good and evil, a confirmation of our confusion only the knowledge of G-d can assuage.

20

Once there was an innocent time when life with G-d was hidden in sweet smoke. The heat of prayerful awareness awoke a thirst in my spirit that could not be quenched by mere love. Led to my root by His messengers and angels, I learned only to thirst for more. On this roadside I sit, weary, parched and parceled, living a dichotomy I cannot embrace, or escape.

21

Who will light the darkened path for our farewell parade with a staff of miracles in his hand? We search all day long for peace on the horizon, the joy of a waltz to rest our soul on, a sleeve for our tears to call home. Yesterday is out there, beyond the edge of this flat world. It travels through today and, overhead it is halfway to its source – the bright light of nightfall that welcomes tomorrow. We have been a nation adrift – abandoned the compass that points the way. We have let them make us endure our enemies long enough. Get ready. It's almost time to go. Our purpose is awaiting our arrival.

ABOUT THE AUTHOR:

Efrayim Levenson is a poet and writing tutor living in Far Rock-away, New York. To support his writing habit he has worked as a heavy-duty truck brake parts rebuilder, a commercial collections specialist, and a law firm accountant. His dream is to be a traveling preacher and hopes his words will lead the way.

Join us on Facebook at Efrayim Levenson
https://www.facebook.com/efrayim.levenson

Other Links:
http://www.efrayimlevenson.com
https://www.amazon.com/author/efrayimlevenson
http://brooklyn.universitytutor.com/tutors/274568
http://www.waterloocottagepress.com

Written correspondence regarding this title may be sent to
efrayimlevenson@gmail.com

Waterloo Cottage Press®
1415A Waterloo Place
Far Rockaway, New York 11691

PUBLISHED BY WATERLOO COTTAGE PRESS®
PRINTED IN THE USA BY CREATESPACE, AN AMAZON COMPANY
For Orders by U.S. trade bookstores and wholesalers,
please visit www.amazon.com

www.ingramcontent.com/pod-product-compliance
Lightning Source LLC
Chambersburg PA
CBHW022351040426
42449CB00006B/824